Victoria Harwood

The Pocket Oracle

550 PREDICTIONS, ADVICE, WORDS OF ENCOURAGEMENT, YOUR HELPER FOR EVERYDAY, UNIQUE EXPERIENCE, MAGIC AND ANSWERS.

WISDOM OF PEOPLE FROM FUTURE

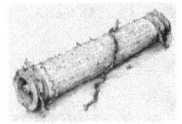

Copyright © 2023 by ViKtoriia Harwood

All rights reserved.

No part of this book may be reproduced in any form or by any electronic or mechanical means, including information storage and retrieval systems, without written permission from the author, except for the use of brief quotations in a book review.

"Life is not merely a matter of passing days, but of making history"
   Ralph Waldo Emerson.

"The world is a huge collection of subjective models of the world. And he tries to correspond to each of them. A great performance, a great power that adapts to what you believe. That's what the game is all about!"
   Radion Marquez

The Oracles

In ancient times, when the gods still communicated with people, there were priests who served as a connection between the heavenly powers and mortals. They were oracles who conveyed predictions on behalf of the deity to those seeking answers and direction in their lives. Majestic temples and sacred places became the arena where these predictions were announced, and people listened to every word with trepidation, considering it an immutable truth.

But oracles were not simply intermediaries between gods and people. They were the source of wisdom and knowledge that permeated their existence. Their judgments and prophecies were recognized as indisputable, and their words influenced the destinies of entire nations

The majestic Oracle of Delphi, sitting in his temple on the slope of Mount Parnassus, was an incomparable master of prediction. Legends say that he conveyed the prophecies of the god Apollo himself, and his words were considered the immutable truth.

But what made him so powerful? Perhaps it was his connection with a mysterious force that chose him as an oracle. And who knows what other powers emanated from his temple, remaining a secret to the oracle himself. Perhaps he himself dreamed of peace and a quiet life, but fate endowed him with an irresistible power to predict the future.

The Delphic Oracle is the embodiment of mystery and wisdom, which has left its mark on history and still delights us with its predictions.

If in the routine of our days we find it difficult to make decisions, we often lack wise advice or moral support. Historically, people have turned to fortune tellers for help and direction but we live in the modern world. Try to get advice and support in your affairs with the help of this book or your intuition!

How to use the Pocket Oracle

To begin, focus on your question and pick up the book. Then, open it at random and read a random page. Trust that your intuition and your higher self, your angels will help you find the right answer for this particular moment, as well as push you in the right direction or warn you against something.

Everything is possible! Believe in yourself, trust yourself and your intuition. I am sure that doors will begin to open to a truer, better path for you

THE POCKET ORACLE

• • •

This method of fortune telling is very ancient. You may or may not believe in this method... And yet, such a simple fortune telling can be useful for those who are looking for new ideas and perspectives, who need support during a long day, support in making decisions, those who are looking for ways of spiritual growth.

Remember, the final choice is always yours. Use predictions as an additional source of information, but trust your intuition and your own mind.

Live with pleasure! May every day make you happy!

Do you want to feel good? – Pick up this book and open it at random!

Want to get moral support before your trip or choice? – open any page without hesitation!

• • •

Do you want to gain perspective from a relationship or situation? – your intuition is looking for an opportunity to tell you! Try using this book to get a message for you!

Are you facing a difficult conversation? – Open the book, scroll through a little, without reading, stop! You will receive a hint on what to do.

Here are more detailed Instruction:

1. Pick up the closed book and get ready for an exciting journey into the world of predictions. Present your question and focus on it for 5 seconds. Allow your energy to interact with your subconscious and higher powers.

2. Now it's time to ask your question out loud or mentally. Feel how your hand begins to move and opens the desired page. This is the magic of the moment when the answer is revealed to you and makes you think.

3. Remember, for each new question you must repeat all previous steps.

. . .

4. You can only ask three questions per day.

5. If you have a digital version of the book, guess the number and open it to the desired page, there will be a message for you.

∼

So, do you have a question that needs an answer?

Get ready for magic. You will open this book to exactly the page with the words you need to hear!

Do not take the prediction-advice literally. Each piece of text contains a key that can open the door that takes you away from problems, onto a clearer path, to new opportunities.

Let the adventure begin!

The Oracles Wisdom

Things, places and details anchor the different stories of our lives. You need to remember a couple of pleasant stories. This will give you the boost you need..

Sometimes your emotions overshadow your common sense. Taking control of your emotions is a wonderful achievement.

Develop unconditional faith in yourself. Believing in yourself is when you keep moving forward even when everyone tells you not to.

You should take care of your diet. Avoid overeating, unhealthy foods and eating when you are not really hungry

Your justice and honesty will be rewarded, despite temporary difficulties.

A leader must at least roughly understand what he wants to get as a result.

Your dream should contain a picture of the goal achieved, and not a scenario and means of achieving it.

Avoid unnecessary spending; you should sort out your finances

Don't waste time on useless activities, concentrate on more important tasks.

The time has come to spend time with your loved ones.

"Reality is something that never was and never will be, but only exists - once and now. Reality exists only for one moment, like a frame on a film that moves from the past to the future." - Vadim Zeland

Do not waste time on unnecessary disputes and conflicts, learn to find compromises and solve problems peacefully

Your love and passion will attract new opportunities and encounters into your life.

Use the "five whys" rule.
See Reference Section at the end of the book - No. 1

You are facing another test; it will help you become stronger. Everything is fine and you are on the right track

You will be able to find harmony and happiness if you live in harmony with nature and accept everything around you as it is

Trust yourself and your intuition.

Change always happens gradually, even from your own point of view.

The instinct of many is to do everything possible to gain recognition from others, but this is an impulse that steals time, energy, mental and physical health.

Your work and efforts will be rewarded. Expect recognition and advancement in your career.

"False beliefs must be weeded out. Then the conscious mind will again begin to perceive its origins and open to the inner channels of greatness and power." Jane Roberts

Your health requires attention

If you need help, ask! One person will refuse, but two will not.

Your creativity will flourish. Don't be afraid to express yourself and share your ideas.

You should be careful with your financial decisions. Try to avoid risky investments.

Start each day with gratitude for what you have. Look what will happen...

"In many cases people know truths that they do not realize intellectually. Since time immemorial they have felt emotionally recharged by storms, and this is, of course, exactly what happens. This process is a constant, necessary and beneficial exchange that results in at least some balance." Jane Roberts

You have the opportunity, there are no guarantees.

Someone needs your support.

I think you will find your own voice in art and more.

Tomorrow is your lucky day!

It's time to think about how to avoid immediate desires.

Your only obligation is to realize that you are the master of your destiny.

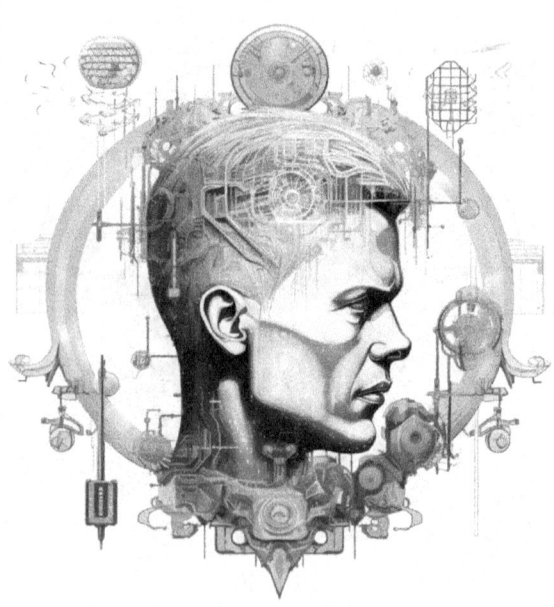

Learn a new hobby and you will find success and satisfaction

All you need in this life is to learn to be happy, regardless of anyone or anything.

Someone you know is sad that you don't write or call. Fix it!

"The power to create your own life resides within you today—from birth and even before." - Jane Roberts

Your energy and good mood are the key to a successful day

Take failures calmly. Every failure is an investment in future success and plus life experience.

Everyone understands - you are the best!

"Pay no attention to those who think you are going crazy, nor to those who tell you that you are making a mistake, nor to those who ask you to go back to the path they think is right. Dream what you want to dream, go where you want to go, be who you are, because life is unique. Remember: you are the door that you have so far been looking for so unsuccessfully." Carl Gustav Jung

Express your opinion whenever asked or necessary. Remember your uniqueness and point of view are valuable

Today is a good day to start something new.

You should go to the mirror and tell your reflection that you love and forgive yourself.

Brainstorm and make a list of all possible solutions to the problem.

May your jokes always bring laughter and joy to those around you. You have a good sense of humour.

Your life will improve, and you will be able to express gratitude and appreciation for the little joys in life. Constantly

Don't doubt your abilities. Rest assured.

The ability to manage your emotions is your main task for the next few days.

Happiness is the ability to accept and appreciate what you have instead of focusing on what you don't have.

Control yourself and hold on! Soon, very soon, it will become easier!

If you need to do something unpleasant, imagine that you are an actor playing a role in a comedy play.

Laughter is the best medicine, so don't hesitate to laugh at yourself and the situations around you.

Consider getting a pet.

"Human life, like any other movement of matter, is a chain of causes and effects. An effect in the space of options is always located close to its cause. Just as one follows from the other, so nearby sectors of space line up in lines of life." - Vadim Zeland

You need a strong, honest and active partner.

You need to create personal boundaries.

Serotonin and dopamine make you happy. - Learn to be proud of yourself! - The principle is that we should be proud of even small victories and actions! Well ... do something that makes you proud.

Today you will be so energetic that you will be able to charge your phone with just your smile.

Any pain goes away. Everything passes and becomes a memory. Think positive.

Imagine the possible consequences of your decision and consider whether you can cope with them.

Ask yourself the question: "Which decision will most maintain my motivation and enthusiasm?"

"The greatest strength is the ability to remain calm within yourself, even when everything around you seem to be chaos." - Dalai Lama

If you want to sleep peacefully, keep your mouth shut.

Wisdom is not knowledge, but the ability to apply knowledge in practical life.

"No apple tree is trying to grow violets." Jane Roberts

In the near future, you will meet a person who will become your reliable friend and support throughout your life

You are loved

The room for growth for each of us lies in improving our greatest strengths

Your creative energy is at its peak, and you will soon create something amazing that will bring you recognition and success.

Being trusted is like finding Eldorado, because from trust comes the confidence that everything is going well and will be fine, this gives rise to a state of lightness, peace and joy

"Be yourself. Take care of yourself, your development. Don't connect your well-being with other people. Create your own world. You don't have to rack your brains to solve problems. Set a goal and move towards it. All problems and contradictions will be resolved along the way, by themselves, one way or another." Vadim Zeland

Love is when you are ready to accept another person with all their shortcomings and mistakes without humiliating yourself and your interests.

Your intuition will be your best advisor, trust it and it will lead to success.

The pain delta is the difference between the level of dissatisfaction with the current situation and the point where a person wants to go.
See Reference Section at the end of the book - No. 4

Your environment will support you and help you achieve your goals. Don't be afraid to ask for help.

While in a subordinate position, note its advantages for yourself. After all, someone else is now "in the line of fire," and you don't have to be responsible for others and worry about defending your position.

Your past will influence your present. Learn from past experiences and use them to develop yourself.

You should be prepared to transform yourself, change, sacrifice and give up in order to achieve your goals. Sometimes you need to let go of the old in order to attract the new.

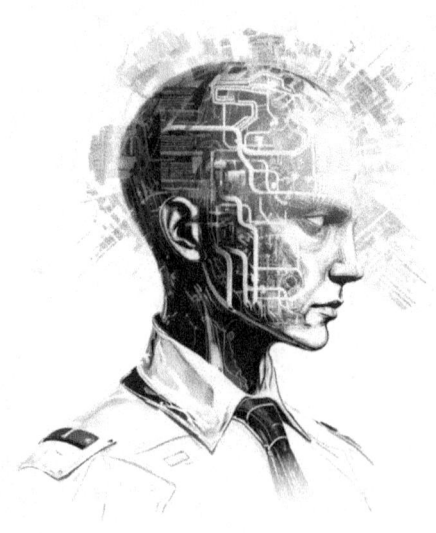

You should turn to your inner sage and find the answers within yourself. The lonely path will lead you to true understanding and enlightenment. Ask yourself more often

"Hating war will not bring peace. Only love for peace can lead to it." Jane Roberts

You should be careful who you trust. Not all people will be sincere and faithful.

Your subconscious mind plays an important role in your life. Be attentive to your dreams and intuition.

"You can't save anyone. You can be present with them, you can offer them your groundedness, your sanity, your peace. You can even share the journey with them, offer them your vision. But you can't take away their pain. You cannot walk their path for them." Jeff Foster

Soon your heart will be filled with love and passion. Open your heart and let love flow into your life.

Your first and last name will have a strong influence on your destiny. Learn the meaning and symbolism of your first and last name. Interesting discoveries await you in your ancestry

You should pay attention to the numbers that constantly attract your attention. They may contain important messages and instructions from your higher self.

Your memory is sharp and reliable, like you have a computer storage system. Use it.

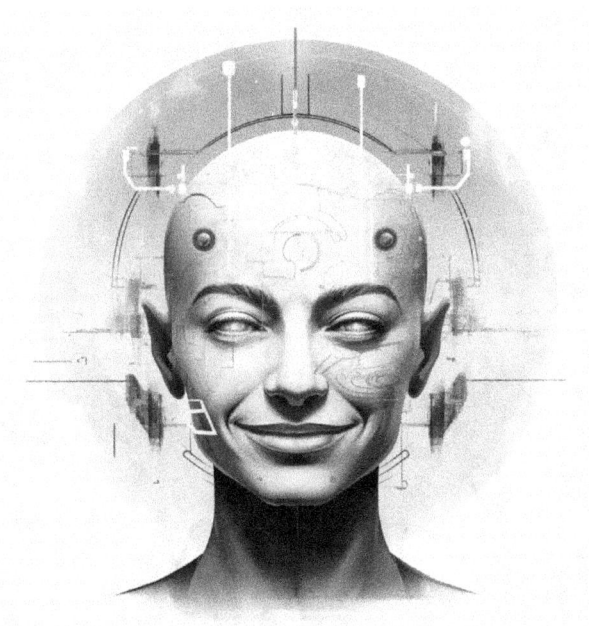

"You are not responsible for what other people expect from you. If they expect too much from you, then it is their fault, not your fault." Richard Feynman

You will be able to avoid all stress and negative emotions this year.

Put yourself in other people's shoes to understand how your decision might affect them.

Next year will bring good luck in your affairs.

Conduct an analysis of potential obstacles and problems to develop a strategy to overcome them.

Trust your intuition and make your decision with the confidence that you have done everything possible to make the right choice.

You should practice listening and being empathetic to other people. Think about it.

Very soon you will have the opportunity to travel. Delve into the features of each new culture, this may be useful to you in the future.

Take a selfie of yourself laughing, look at the photo from time to time

"Silence of the mind is beauty in itself. To listen to a bird, to the voice of a man, to the speech of a politician or a priest, to all the continuous noise of propaganda, to listen in complete silence is to hear much more, to see much more." Jiddu Krishnamurti

There are people who know how to love for nothing...

Be prepared for unexpected turns of events that can lead to new opportunities and successes.

I am lucky in all my affairs; luck is always with me!
Everything that happens to me happens for the better!

You will find new ways to be happy and experience deep joy in your life.

It is important to learn to live in the present moment and enjoy every day.

Be ready for a little adventure.

Don't put off important things until tomorrow. Do them today

If a goal seems unattainable, change your action plan. Believe in yourself!

The future promises prosperity and financial stability.

No one can stop you while you pursue your dreams.

Stop! Look at the situation from a different angle. You will find an unexpected solution

"If you think about obstacles for a long time, you will run into them. You must mentally create a new picture. It will differ from that which is conveyed by the physical senses at any given time, and precisely in those areas where changes are necessary." Jane Roberts

You are loved and the best thing you can do for yourself is to be happy.

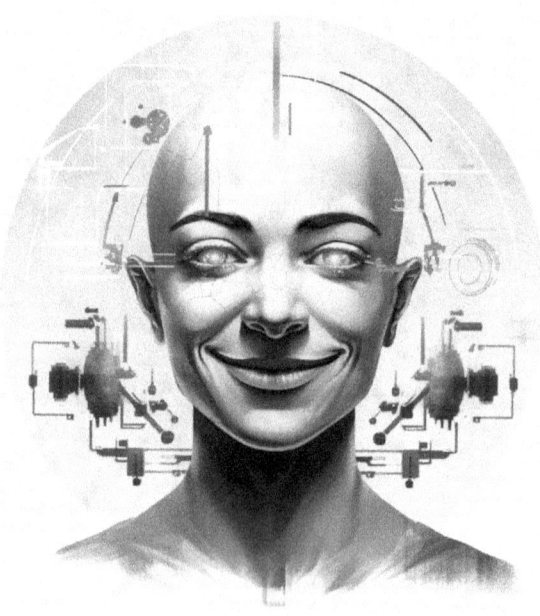

By going through this experience, you will become a better version of yourself.

"Your happiness cannot come from outside."
See Reference Section at the end of the book - No. 5

Your love life is about to change. Perhaps meeting a new partner or strengthening relationships with an existing one

Do things that make you laugh or be with people who make you laugh - laughter is a very high vibrational energy, even if we are laughing at ourselves!

Happiness is something you create within yourself, not something you look for outside.

Happiness is a state of mind, it does not come from things

Fortune favours the brave! Laugh at difficulties and everything will work out for you.

Learn to surrender and you will see how beautifully your destiny will lead you to a better place.

Disappointment be damned! Charm sounds better!

Remember who you are and what you believe in. This will help you overcome any difficulties in life.

Repeat to yourself over and over again: I love myself! I forgive myself! I believe in myself!

It's time to stop pretending all the time, be yourself occasionally. This has its own charm.

It is impossible to be good to everyone. Don't try, do the best you can. Remember about yourself.

You are going in the right direction. Good luck!

It's not time yet, this door will open for you on its own at the right time

Look for resources within yourself, you have them and get enough sleep!

You are full of life and enthusiasm, especially next week.

By developing a positive mindset, you attract the best for yourself into your life.

Focus on finding opportunities, this will help you find the right path

"Listen to your own thoughts that arise in the process of life. What ideas are you putting into your head? Understand: they are the ones that will materialize in your life." Jane Roberts

Being offended is not the best solution. It's time to grow up and try to see the situation as a whole, draw conclusions, this will help you move forward.

The world loves you and only wants the best for you.

Face your fears and see them as opportunities for spiritual development

You shouldn't chase small gains.

You are a smart, handsome adult, responsible and adequate person.

Play with your pets – Our pets teach us a lesson about unconditional love, which always raises your positive vibrations and gives us strength.

You have the right to make a choice at any time. Believe in the best!

Recipe for Trust: Protection, contact, energy, perseverance —> Trust.

Sometimes blind luck leads to success. You have to experience it for yourself.

You always have a choice! Make one!

Be patient. Success and luck are on your side.

Leave grudges behind and rise above it. Smile and the world around you will begin to change.

Your dreams will come true very soon.

Excessive rationalism kills the magic of life.

It's time to go with a friend to a bar with other friends.

Things are going well, follow your heart.

Your potential and possibilities are limitless. Remember this

Set ambitious goals, dream! Dreams do come true.

Be careful with your thoughts, not all of them are yours, some are imposed.

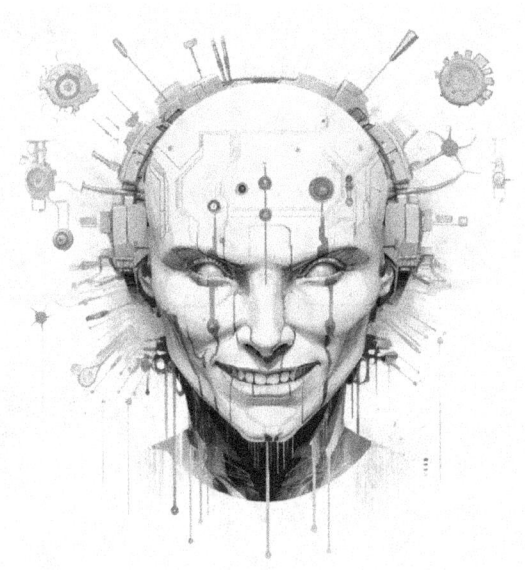

Practice self-analysis and reflection to understand your strengths and weaknesses

It's time for you to start painting. Start sketching.

The greatest wisdom is understanding that we are still learning and growing.

You can find a solution for any difficult situation.

To be a kind person all the time, good contact with your power is important.

You have to create your own happiness. No one will do this for you

Maintain a balance between work and rest.

Take care and appreciate yourself! You are the best you have

When in a dominant position, enjoy the respect of others and the opportunity to choose rather than feel pressure from outside.

You have a great immune system, talk to it! Health is important.

Accept that you can't control everything around you.
See Reference Section at the end of the book - No. 3

Try to look at the world through rose-coloured glasses sometimes - literally or figuratively. Is it worth being so materialistic?

Time to relax and watch a good movie. Everything else can wait.

True friends will always be by your side.

Buy yourself a cake!

Challenge yourself to find at least one thing where you can laugh. Laugh more often!

I am a person; I shape my physical environment. I change and create my own world. I am free from space and time. I am part of everything that exists. There is no place inside me where there is no creation!

Today you will make only the right decisions! Rest assured.

It's time to say "no" to the manipulations of your neighbours

"You have the right to be, to exist, to feel what you feel, to think what you think. You have the right to joy and the right to sadness. And the right to doubt too." - Jeff Foster

Take advantage of the advice you will receive today. It will help you

Imagine that you are speaking in front of a large audience. You are doing everything right.

A meeting with long-awaited success awaits you, but they happen to be 15 minutes late.

Very soon you will be proud of someone close to you.

A vase in your home stands waiting for beautiful colours. Is it not?

The ability to defend oneself and a deep sense of the right to defend oneself is the absolute foundation needed to go out into the world beyond one's home.

An unusual gift from fate awaits you - a pack of cookies in which all the predictions will come true. We need to find it. Intuition will tell you where.

Go for a walk, the fresh air and the sound of trees will restore your strength. Sit on a park bench and look at the clouds floating across the sky.

Be patient and kind to yourself. Everyone makes mistakes

Forgive yourself.

Take everything you need, it's a gift from fate.

Once you become aware of your weaknesses, you will become stronger.

"Take yourself a target thought form: I am the master of my consciousness; the control panel is in my hands; I and only I decide which buttons to press; I control my thoughts; I have a clean and clear mind; I can do everything; I reign supreme in my kingdom; The Force is with me." Vadim Zeland

You will be able to meet the person of your dreams very soon

If you have a great goal in front of you, but your opportunities are limited, go for it anyway.

"There are two ways to express yourself - authentic and strategic. Authentic – showing who you really are. Strategically - impersonating someone else for profit. Anyone who follows a strategic path sooner or later discovers that all the benefits that appear to him are not actually received by him, but by an image, a ghost, which he himself created." Robert Reznik

These people will not stand on ceremony. Be careful.

Express gratitude - be grateful for the beauty around you, even if it is a small tree in the middle of a big city. Be grateful for the food you are about to eat and everything else that has blessedly come into your life, including something negative that turns out to be a wonderful life lesson that expands your spiritual growth.

Tomorrow will be a bright spot if life seems sad to you right now

Very soon you will catch up on what you missed.

Every challenge is an opportunity for development, and success will follow.

Is everything you dream about really necessary?

Watch children play - try to remember the charm of the first sensation and the innocence of childhood.

"You create your personal reality through conscious beliefs about yourself, others, and the world at large." - Jane Roberts

Ask yourself: "Which decision aligns with my values and principles?"

Follow your emotions and intuition, but don't rely on them alone. Combine them with logical thinking.

The secret is that fe   person's positive energy but allow them to be controlled by those who impose them.

Set your priorities, you will understand what is most important to you in reality.

Keep your plans a secret until you make them happen!

Low energy vibrations can control our lives. Remember this

Plan your time and write a to-do list for the next day, you will be more organized.

Don't build a ceremony where they won't be appreciated. Say what you think needs to be said.

If you show the world that your boundaries can be pushed through, then you begin to attract many people who want to do this.

You'll find new ways to express your creativity and attract the people you want. How do you feel about popularity?

Is it so important to have a lot of money in your account? Maybe just enough for all your plans?

Tomorrow, take everything calmly, no matter what happens. It will pass, as everything passes in life. A new chapter will begin.

To love is to accept the person you love as he is with all its pros and cons and remain yourself!

If you need to relax, try making a silly face in front of the mirror - it's guaranteed to make you smile.

Conduct a SWOT analysis to assess your own strengths and weaknesses to understand what direction to take next.

You were born to be happy. All the rest does not matter. That's worth thinking about.

It's time to prioritize and write down your real dreams and desires on a piece of paper.

Think about what you can do to make you feel better?
Maybe just sincerely talk to yourself, find reasons?

The past is gone, it is no more. There is no future yet. Live in the present, for the moment and appreciate it. There is a lot in the world that you can sincerely rejoice at.

Forgive yourself and others - none of us are perfect; there are those who have hurt us and those who have been hurt by us. Forgive them, but don't forget to forgive yourself too.

Take care of yourself! Think about what you want. Leave others their problems. This is the key to happiness.

"Change, as you must know, involves not only growth, but also complete disorientation to make room for another, perhaps newer orientation. You see the realization of values in terms of growth, and therefore you think of decay in terms of psychic destruction and death. That is, you see the end as a consequence of any beginning." Jane Roberts

Don't be satisfied with what's the leas bad. You deserve better.

Appreciate your loved ones, this is your rear.

"To get rid of anxiety about a reality that you cannot change, you need to accept it." Vadim Zeland.
See Reference Section at the end of the book - No. 7

Sleep and rest are what you need. Preferably by the sea.

Imagine the possible consequences of your decision and consider whether you can cope with them.

Tomorrow it's better for you to take a break from all your activities

You should write down on a piece of paper all the pros and cons of the upcoming decision, then you will be sure that this is exactly what you need.

Keep your plans secret!

It is all in your hands.

You will have the opportunity to enjoy the moment and learn to appreciate the simple pleasures of life.

Learn to take responsibility and be responsible for your actions

You will be able to create a harmonious relationship if you treat your partner with respect.

After the rain, the sun will appear from behind the clouds. Smile

What's the point in dreaming, it's time to act.

Observe your ill-wisher, what his weaknesses are, what his strengths are. Use them.

It's time to learn something new. Or find an interesting book

If a person is not eager to meet, this is not your person. Look for those who are interested in you.

Persistence is an excellent quality in certain matters. Everything needs balance.

"Your happiness is not a state, not a passing experience, not an experience, and not a feeling that others can give you. Your happiness is the boundless, omnipresent, unlimited space of the heart, in which joy and sadness, bliss and melancholy, confidence and doubt, loneliness and "connectedness," even fear and strong desire, can replace each other, like rainy and sunny weather." Jeff Foster

If you manage to change your beliefs and views, the scenery will change.

You need to help if you are asked for help.

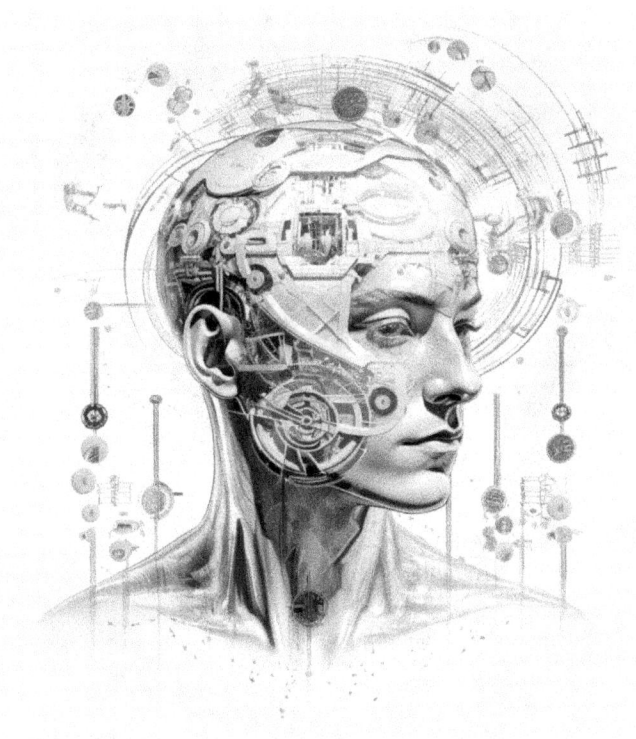

You should not make very high demands on life. The higher your status, the more self-discipline.

Don't hesitate!

People are divided into two groups: those who serve themselves and those who serve others. Where do you stand?

Sometimes you have to regret what it took so long to achieve

You are part of the world around you and the World loves you

I think you need to master a set of physical exercises and do them.

Dancing just 10 minutes a day is the key to health for many years.

You create enthusiasm around you.

"The conscious mind is given to you for a reason. You are not at the mercy of unconscious urges unless you consciously give in to them. You can use your current feelings and desires to check your development at any time. If you don't like your own feelings, then you should change the nature of your conscious thoughts and expectations. You must change the colour of the messages that your thoughts convey to your body, friends and acquaintances." Jane Roberts

A person is responsible for the energy that they project into the world and into their own state. That is, the vibrations of their thoughts, emotions, moods and actions are reflected both in the quality of their own life and in everything that surrounds them.

Live your own life. Why do you need the events of the outside world?

Be brave, everything is in your hands.

Be grateful for your body

Open yourself up to new ideas, they will change your life for the better.

You are your own source of inspiration and energy.

This day and tomorrow are ideal to take on a challenging task

You can do it. Dare to try.

Trust what happens to you.

Learn a new task. This will give you a surge of strength.

Be prepared for changes in your relationship. Some people may leave your life, but new important connections will appear.

Take life easier! Life is a great show put on in your honour.

It's time to go into the forest, into nature, to hear the birds singing and the trees rustling.

Life is a path between the past and the future.
 Where are you in your thoughts? It's time to live in the present!

When your partner is crying, you are losing money!

If you feel impatient or angry, just roll your eyes counterclockwise and it will go away.

Despair will not help you, look for other emotions. A new state gives birth to new connections.

Think about how to remove worry from your life. Maybe we should trust life, people, the world more?

Soon you will have a long journey that will open up new perspectives

Anxiety is draining. Why do you need these emotions and loss of energy?

Don't judge others but accept people as they are. Learn the best from each person and leave them to their own devices. By judging, you take on the worst in them. Everyone has their own path.

Give yourself a day off, go to the theatre, museum, or exhibition. Where the soul calls.

To be ruthless is a violation of the harmony between gentleness and cruelty

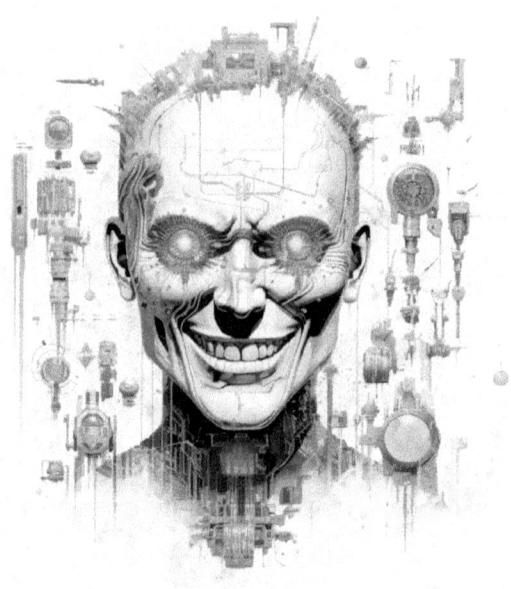

Egoism and Altruism. Like all opposites like Yin and Yang. Look for a middle ground.

Find ways to take better care of yourself.

Some people are like springs of clean water.
You will soon meet one of them.

Accepting yourself, other people and the world unconditionally is a task worth working on.

You are on the right track.

Opening the heart is the main key to awakening deep awareness

Don't insist on being in control. Let everything be as it is. Many surprises await you.

"Every time I wake up in the morning I become better and better in every way."

"There is a possibility that children who forget to call home do not grow up with age." - Zakhartseva

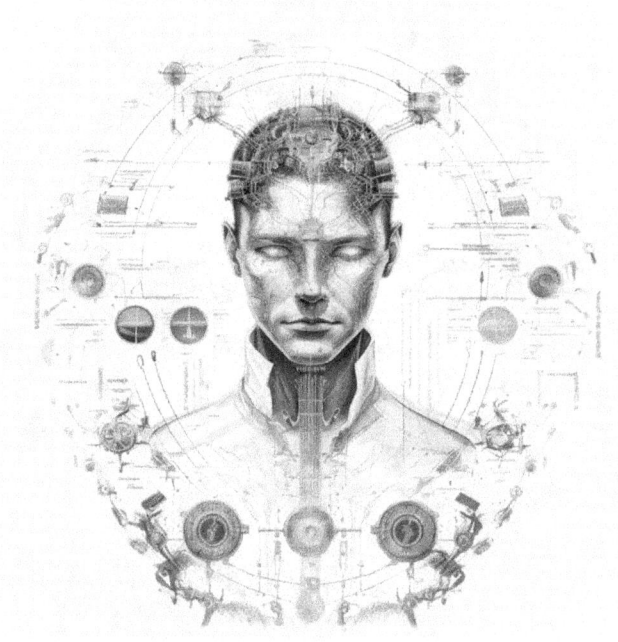

Feelings and thoughts are free to arise and disappear as if I were not their cause.

"You may partially understand the nature of reality and complain: I am sure that I create problems for myself, but I am completely unable to change it. If this is the case, then - no matter what you tell yourself - you still could not believe that you yourself are the creator of your own existence. Once you accept this fact, you can immediately begin to change what makes you unhappy or irritated."

Jane Roberts

Sometimes you can just take off into the clouds and intuitively move towards your goal.

The soul is the level of our sincere feelings, true desires, emotions and needs. Remember this often.

The Higher Self is experienced as an intuitively felt inner potential. For some reason, it still needs to be updated and become itself.

Be with someone who makes you feel good. Work where you are comfortable and interested in working.

How much money in your account do you need to be happy? Can you answer right away? Multiply this number by 10!

Appreciate your uniqueness and talents.

If you feel sad, repeat the following words out loud: joy, love, gratitude, happiness, tenderness, miracle, desires, sun, smile, gifts, easy, I can, light, hug, kiss, friendship, family, wealth, holiday, beautiful, wonderful, warm, pleasant, brilliant, it will work out, support, inspiration, purity, freshness, confidence, kindness.

"Only by renouncing its functions does consciousness surrender itself to the power of 'negative' experience. Only by refusing responsibility does it surrender itself to the mercy of events over which it supposedly has no control." Jane Roberts

For a week, write down every experience that brought you pleasure! This way you will attract something important into your life.

Maybe you should be alone, alone with yourself, at least for a few days?

Change your strict daily routine at least for one day. Feel how easy it is to live.

"Letting go of someone is much easier than doing the same for yourself." Max Fry

Don't put what you have to do on someone else's shoulders. You need to experience it yourself.

Do you have your own home, a place where you feel safe, cozy and comfortable?

Soon you will meet a clear-eyed stranger who can become your great friend if you are lucky enough to meet them.

As long as a person is alive, nothing is missing. There is always a way out of any situation, and not just one, but several...

I don't like harmful, dulling or lulling lies.

Human life is completely unpredictable. Appreciate those who are close to you.

Your home is where your heart is.

If you are open to new opportunities and ready to take action, anything is possible.

"If the importance cannot be reset, then it is necessary to let go of the grip of control over the situation and move from worries to active actions. Just start taking action, somehow. It doesn't matter how, whether it's effective or not. Allow yourself to act out badly. The potential for importance will be dissipated in the process of movement, the energy of intention will be released, and you will succeed." Vadim Zeland

Every day is a new start. Don't get attached to what happened yesterday.

You will have as much success as you want.

You have to do a complex task that you don't know how to approach, break the task into many subtasks.

Don't take anything for free unless you want to spend extra money.

Step by step and you will reach your goal.

Allow yourself to be 'ungrateful, 'ill-mannered', 'crazy' or a 'bitch' on occasion - if this is the price of freedom.

Be free. Bless yourself. Play everything you have.

Add a little tenderness to your day.

Your patience pays off!

Instead of thinking 'what if', think 'next time'.

By focusing on the bad or sad, the mind will begin to focus your attention on negative and destructive situations

Write down and implement plans. A surge of strength and desire to live awaits you.

Good news is on its way to you.

Always believe that everything will be fine for you. It will be so. And pain is a process of transformation.

In any unfamiliar place, forget about your fine organization and try to determine the degree of real danger and a way out of it, if something happens.

Try to give yourself an honest answer about what you want. Abstract yourself from public opinion that imposes desires on you

Stop complaining about your problems and start solving them.

Each of us is new to this wonderful world.

"You are beautiful in your imperfections, outrageously perfect in your doubts, loved even in your inability to love. All these parts of you are a given, they are all part of the whole, and you have never been less than the whole." Jeff Foster

Take the opportunity to be surprised by all the details of the day, this will help you look at the world and your surroundings differently, with different eyes.

Humans have the ability to control the forces of nature through mental concentration and altered states of consciousness, merging the sensation of their body with earthly vibrations

Not deciding is also a decision. Not changing is also a choice. If you make that choice, be with it.

Celebrate every unique moment of your life.

You will be outstanding and successful in your career.

Love yourself the way you want to be loved.

Refuse to communicate with those who always criticize and are always dissatisfied with everything.

Marriage does not save you from problems, or from emptiness, or from loneliness.

We pull out all our internal objections in order to go out and doing something cool.

The quality of your life depends on the quality of your thoughts

Today is your day of luck! Take advantage of this.

Write a list of wishes, the most incredible ones that will never come true
Re-read in a year.

Every day, every minute your life gets better and better.

Listen to classical music or go to a concert.

Everything you need: your strength, courage, compassion and love - you already have it all.

You can score a goal! Stay alert.

The desire for power is generated by a feeling similar to childhood anger, which is based on fear.

If you always look for approval and encouragement from others, you will never be able to feel happy.

Gratitude increases levels of dopamine and serotonin, neurotransmitters responsible for feelings of joy and happiness

There will never be complete clarity. Don't wait for it, get used to acting in conditions of partial uncertainty.

Find a secluded place and shout at the top of your lungs several times. This will bring relaxation and relief.

Don't focus on the negative, think about what you are grateful for.

Think about where and how to boost your energy. This will come in handy in the near future.

The tone and health of the physical body is a prerequisite for spiritual health. Think about it!

People don't change, they just take off their masks.

"You have a right. The right to be right and wrong, the right to this gigantic happiness that you knew when you were little. You breathe, and you are inseparable from the life force that "animates" everything, reveals itself in every moment of this incredibly wonderful, amazing existence." - Jeff Foster

Don't dwell on the past and don't dream about the future. Find your passion now and go for it.

Restore your peace of mind and everything will work out on its own. I assure you!

Your financial situation will improve if you continue to work at it.

No spiritual practice will save you from real problems. solve problems of the objective real world in this reality with specific actions.

Treat yourself well, love, forgive. You deserve the best.

Find time, go to the theatre. Acting will help you understand something important.

Write a plan for the next day in the evening, this will increase your productivity.

Do what you did at the very beginning of your relationship and it will never end.

Precision, attention to detail and respect are all required during the building phase of your life. Thoughtfulness breeds clarity

An important meeting for you is coming up on Wednesday

Anxiety, internal struggle, guilt, sadness and regrets appear when a person stops living in the present.

If you look through the eyes of love, everything looks different.

Remember all the similar promises you made to yourself and others and decide what to do with them.

Your values are the guideline for choosing your calling in life

You live in accordance with invisible laws. And when you feel these invisible fundamental laws, synchronize with them, then visible and invisible forces turn on to help you, then everything becomes possible.

Dance is an expression of emotions and feelings. It allows us to release stress and negative emotions and communicate joy and happiness through body movement. Dance every day!

"Fear knocked, Love answered, but there was no one at the door."

You live by the fruits of your actions, and your actions are the result of your thoughts. Filter your thoughts!

Learn to admit your mistakes.

Try practicing Matthew's Principle.
See Reference Section at the end of the book - No. 2

Do what you like. Why put off going to the theatre, fishing or traveling until retirement?! Pamper yourself. Spend your time and energy on things that will fulfil you

"Seven doors are locked with seven keys." - Natalia Zakhartseva

A journey of a thousand miles begins with one step. This step will lead you to opportunities you never knew existed

Track down your affections, treat them without zeal. You don't own anything.

He who seeks finds.

You have a friendly heart and are admired.

You are charming and exciting.

Stop trying to control everything.

Buy flowers for yourself or for somebody.

Design your ideal life. What is your ideal life?

Learn to accept what is happening to you, rather than fight it.

All past events were given to you in order to gain experience and wisdom.

The main goal is to always be at peace with yourself, and not what you thought.

If you can become more accepting of others, they will in turn begin to accept you.

Live the way you want, and don't compare your happiness with others.

You need to be sure that your potential, emotional, intellectual and physical capabilities are inexhaustible.

Meditation heals the soul.

When others participate in your success, you gain true allies

You were created for success, and don't let anyone convince you otherwise. Success is, first of all, great achievements and enjoyment of life.

Everything is temporary.

Turn your calling into money.

"You have been given a great gift to live. You have the ability to contemplate and feel. You are given the opportunity to hear music and see the smile of your loved one. You have been given the opportunity to walk barefoot on soft grass and swim in mighty rivers. Birds and fish live next to you. You have everything to love and give love. There is so much room for joy in you. You have the sun and millions of stars. You have everything and you are everything. You are life and you can give life. It's wonderful that you exist. Look how much you have!!"

Vadim Zeland

You have the right to follow your own path.

You have to try everything in life. To know what to refuse

Values guide your decisions. Decisions shape destiny.

You can look at everything differently and understand how insignificant life's troubles are on the scale of a lifetime

It's better to do something stupid than to do nothing at all!

If you have illusions that with the birth of a child your life will smell like roses, think carefully about whether you should have children at all.

Relationships are a mutual responsibility, and if everyone is responsible for themselves, not their partner.

Tomorrow will be tomorrow, turn your attention to today

Relax, dream about what you really want. And you will get it.

Know how to give up unnecessary things.

Life sees you as you are from the inside and not the way you want to appear to life and the people around you. Be grateful.

Don't take life so seriously. Much is out of your control. Become an observer.

No one intends to harm you. Your pictures of the world just don't match.

Now everything will go according to your wishes.

There is no need at all to participate in everything that comes to your attention.

What roles do you play in your life? I think you are very mobile and a versatile explorer. A new role awaits you.

Laugh at yourself, at your behaviour. In general, laugh a lot.

Anything is possible if you just believe in it.

It's not necessary to feel needed. You need yourself first of all.

The easiest way to raise your feelgood factor is with positive thoughts

If you and your partner don't have anything in common from the very beginning, then it's unlikely to appear.

Turn envy into a positive way, you just want to have even better things

Your intuition is your inner navigator, and when you are connected to it, it can guide you down the right path almost effortlessly. Listen to it.

What a person does is more important than what they talk about

It is your choice whether to focus on the positive or negative traits of the interlocuter.

If you do the main thing, that is, recognize yourself in all the actions and movements of the world through you, then everything works out by itself.

Problems and happiness have no relationship. Become a happy person.

If you feel like you've reached a dead end while solving a problem, give yourself some time, get bored. A solution will pop into your head unexpectedly.

"Are you desperate to achieve your goal? Stop wishing, you will get what you want. Just think about what you are taking. Take it calmly, without demanding or insisting. After all, I want this, so what's the matter? I will have it. " Vadim Zeland

New experiences and new friends will enrich your life.

Every action has consequences. Maybe you don't foresee everything but try to analyse the best you can. The better you imagine your options, the smarter your behaviour.

Your life will soon become even more interesting.

Treat enemies and well-wishers normally, they motivate.

Any thought that arises in your brain and takes hold there will have an impact on your life. Think positively.

It can happen that the door opens into a dark forest. Be prepared

Take criticism as advice to do something better.

Reality exists only in the form in which it appears to you.

You will easily jump up in the morning - and life will sparkle with all sorts of colours!

Irritation is a sign of internal dissatisfaction. Do you always do what you want?

You always have a choice.

Relationships provide us with the most important spiritual lessons in life. You need to learn to give and love unconditionally.

We suffer when we fight reality.

We adopt the qualities of the person we criticize or praise

Friendly conversation can break down barriers, it's worth a try

If you have a feeling of guilt ingrained inside you, life will find a way to "punish" you. Forgive yourself! Repeat "I forgive myself" over and over again.

Give yourself time to laugh, play, have fun! You deserve the best.

Accept yourself as you are.

Dance! Dance helps you express your individuality. It allows each person to find their own unique style and way of expression, which promotes the development of self-expression and self-identity.

Do you want to change your circumstances? Start thinking and approaching things a little differently.

Pride instils dignity in you.

Be sure to buy some tea, you can right now. Guests are on the doorstep

Look for the reasons for your anger, maybe you are angry from internal dissatisfaction.

There is a reason for everything and nothing happens by chance. Everything that happens is for the better.

The essence of any addiction, in emotionally tense situations, is the desire to find support with artificial means such as nicotine, alcohol, drugs.

The most important decision you can make is to be happy no matter what.

"Aesculapius removes his braid. Not today, buddy." – Natalia Zakhartseva

Everything that is made with skill and love bears a special imprint of that standard of living, where money is spent on things more valuable than money.

Do something unusual! Paint a wall, make a collage of wallpaper, cross-stitch initials on towels, engrave a design on a wooden table. All this has much more power than it seems at first glance.

Every thought you think and every decision you make comes from your beliefs and values.

Don't be kind, be objective, forgiving and fair.

All restrictions are only in your head.

When you have contact with the world, your desires and decisions are automatically congruent with the desires and intentions of the larger system around you, including the intentions of nature.

Our life values make us free.

Be silent more and talk less. Especially about your life.

Don't make a hasty decision. Sit down, listen to good music, eat good food, smile and give yourself time to think

Often a simple touch can be more effective than a half-hour conversation.

Don't argue, leave your opponent to your opinion. You won't be able to convince him.

You should love honesty more than money.

Learn from criticism. Criticism is something that can teach you to be better.

Every person you meet on your life's path is a reflection of some part of yourself. Watch the people around you and you will understand your mistakes.

Be aware that other people may have different views on the situation

When you start fighting for a joyful, interesting life, not everyone will be ready to follow you.

Quit a job you don't like or learn to enjoy it, no matter what it is.

Great, you're open to new things.

Do what you wanted and dreamed of doing since childhood. Master the guitar, piano, vocals, skiing, watercolour painting, mosaic, clay, anything you wish.

The most valuable thing you have is your time and energy, since both of these substances are limited.

The truth is that you are not for everyone and not everyone is for you.

Let go of people who are not ready to love you.

Dancing improves memory and concentration. It requires memorizing movements and combinations, which helps develop brain activity and improve cognitive functions

It's time to let off steam and allow yourself to raise your voice.

Stop having difficult conversations with people who don't want to change.

Learn to say "no!".

Focus on what is important at the moment, this will help restore clarity of thought.

Put yourself in someone else's shoes. Try to see life from another person's perspective

You will need to move through and let go of the rage, sadness and pain. You will have to soften, open your heart, start trusting life.

No sacrifice is justified.

Don't talk bad about others.

Don't lie to yourself. Learn to understand yourself. Be aware of your true needs and feelings. And think about how it will be better for you.

Do what makes you happy. Or do everything with joy. This will improve your quality of life.

If there is a high level of aggression in the subconscious, life will "attack" you. Think about how to reduce this level.

Dance at home alone or with someone. Dance relieves stress, improves mood and increases self-esteem.

Go to the mirror, look into the eyes of your reflection and say: "You are the best!" You can even wink!

Try to do something differently today than you always have. Go down a new road, buy something you've never bought before, start talking to a stranger.

You deserve real love.

Sunday is your lucky day.

Have a serious conversation with yourself about goals and desires, no matter how vague.

Circumstances are controlled only through managing your own states.

Climb at least some peak, feel what it's like to be on top. A roof will do too.

You will climb the ladder of professional success and reach the top

What do you think about most of the time? Set priorities based on the needs of the present moment.

Outline 3-5 areas in which you would like to change your life in 5-10 years.

Rational people do not believe in inspiration, for which they often pay with a feeling of boredom and all sorts of other negative conditions

It's time for you to go on vacation. How about a cruise?

Learn to accept what you don't agree with.

Leave relationships that are not helping you.

World is not fair. There are no guaranteed ways to succeed and no guaranteed way to avoid failure.

Pain is inevitable, suffering is your personal choice.

"The problem only arises when there is a desire for results. When the search for a result stops, only then there are no problems." Jiddu Krishnamurti

Forgive others and people will become more forgiving of your mistakes

What is fully understood will not be repeated.

Get rid of the habit of delaying making decisions. 9 out of 10 opportunities are missed due to delay in taking action

Develop yourself and train your brain. Try to identify your weaknesses and develop them.

Can you imagine how unhappy they are?

Observe your thoughts and emotions, not judging them as good or bad, but simply paying attention to them—letting them be without doing anything about them.

Create a passive income.

At the end of each day, write down at least one thing for which you can sincerely thank: yourself, the people you interacted with during the day, and the world in general.

Be honest with yourself.

Hug the person you love.

Of course, it is important to learn to respect boundaries in a gentle and kind way. But it happens in different ways

From good contact with your power, a sense of security is born and true kindness becomes possible.

You can only trust yourself 100%.

The mind is only an instrument of perception. It can control a lot. It can be trained and improved.

You are great and you are doing everything right!

Write a letter to your future self. What would you do if you were 10 years wiser?

Why are you looking for attention? Because you are not confident in yourself, you don't know who you are. Think about how to fix this.

Fall in love

You are a separate person, you should not love what others love, you have every right to live without authority. You will also be responsible for your choice.

Do you want to win the lottery? Wait until midnight, close your eyes and imagine the numbers in front of your mind's eye. You only need to write down the second fifth and sixth of those that you see.

The core of maturity: Just because it's not your fault doesn't mean it's not your responsibility.

Add a little more creativity to what you do.

Play with yourself and the world, and people will join in and ask to play your games.

Think about what you can do today that will improve the world

The 'I love you' stage ends quickly. If you haven't learned to talk, respect, and care for each other, then you should not have got into a relationship.

Live in pleasure! Do everything for fun.

Remove the unimportant. Understand the short-term nature of things like status, fame, recognition.

Don't be afraid to ask questions.

Try to find the 20/80 path. Minimum effort, but maximum result.

Your love life will blossom and you will have a romantic adventure that will rock your world.

By being aware of your weaknesses and understanding what you want to achieve, you are much more likely to achieve success.

It is impossible to overdo gratitude; it is pure magic, truly a magic word.

Your imagination knows no bounds

You have an excellent ability to adapt to any changes and difficulties

What kind of trust can we talk about if you have a chronic feeling of insecurity?

Focus on creating, not consuming.

Very soon, without any reason, you will feel happier than ever before in your life, you will feel that everything is in its place, that there are no mistakes anywhere.

If you have fears inside, life will scare you. And vice versa

You are beautiful. You are very smart. You are wonderful. If someone doesn't understand this, that's their problem.

Make new acquaintances. This will open up new opportunities for you

Sometimes each of us needs to stop, relax and let off steam.

We often forget the fact that our speech is not only a way of expressing thoughts, but also an energetic "charge" that has suggestion, influence and mood. Words have tremendous power.

Forgive those who ask for forgiveness.

"Symbolic violence" is when people stop wanting what they actually want and begin to want what is declared as desirable, distributed as examples of the desired lifestyle.

"Give up worry, desire and hope. Leave only calm confidence." - Vadim Zeland.
See Reference Section at the end of the book - No. 8

Tell your loved ones more often that you love them.

Don't be the best. Be unique.

Trust cannot be copied. You can't buy it and it cannot be downloaded

Dance today, now! Dance brings joy and satisfaction. It allows us to enjoy the moment, forget about everyday problems and simply enjoy movement and music.

You are only limited by your own thoughts and beliefs.

Happiness does not depend on what you have, but on how you look at what you have.

Why do you need perfection? Just live, breathe evenly, deeply

For some reason, the World around you does not stand up for you... Your World is a mirror and reflects your attitude towards yourself.

"Have you ever tried to sit completely still, without the slightest movement of your body, including without moving your eyes? Sit like this for two minutes. During this time, everything will be revealed to you - if you know how to look." - Jiddu Krishnamurti

THE POCKET ORACLE

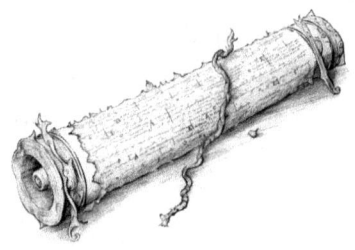

References

1.

The Five WHYs Method

"The founder of Toyota, Sakichi Toyoda, constantly used the "five whys" rule. In all incomprehensible situations, he used this method, and it always helped him. This is an example of the rule:

You want a fur coat.

Ask yourself: why do I want a fur coat?

This is the first "why".

You answer: because I want to surprise everyone.

Okay, second "why":

Why do you want to surprise everyone?

Answer: because I want to be noticed.

Third "why":

Why do you need to be noticed? Answer: because I feel insecure.

Fourth "why":

Why do you feel insecure?

Answer: because I can't realize myself, because I'm sitting in one place.

Fifth "why":

Why can't you realize yourself?

Answer: because I'm doing something I don't like.

And tell me now, what does the fur coat have to do with it?"

2.

Matthew's Principle

The Bible says: "...to him who has, more will be given and he will have abundance, but whoever does not have, even what he has will be taken away from him." Add everything, both "good" and "bad". For all small problems and pleasures, say to yourself: "It counts", "Plus", "Fortunately", "Well, good, and this is in the piggy bank", "Everything is for the better." And notice how things begin to change for the better.

3.

The brain likes to keep everything under control, but this cannot always be done, and it is important to learn to let go of control. To do this, learn to do it in small ways - if you always make your bed - try not to do this for a couple of weeks).

4.
"The more painful it is for a person to see his current standard of living compared to his desired one, the more demands he has on how quickly he must move forward. In this case, the paradoxical mechanism "in spite of the conductor I will walk" is activated. If I cannot get everything at once, then I will not humiliate myself and engage in this nonsense. This is all below me. Read "it makes me more painful to realize that I can't have everything I want today". Then this delta of pain turns into an internal critic who begins to mercilessly torment you from within, demanding that you get up and run a marathon right away. People who have achieved a lot in life also have an inner critic, but it may have a different message. It's more about comparison, your own inadequacy, which is not as good as you wanted. But for people who have achieved little or are doing little now, the inner critic = the level of self-hatred = self-directed delta of pain = despair from the difference between the desired life and the current one can simply go off scale. And what's surprising is that being under the yoke of a critic day after day turns out to be easier than lowering your expectations a little and "lowering yourself to small steps." After all, until you

lower the bar, there is always hope that one day you will get up and realize that you already have level C 3. And lowering the bar to 10 minutes every day is like giving up, losing, coming to terms with your miserable life for the rest of your days. Because that's exactly how the internal distorting mirror works. " (author unknown)

5.

"Your happiness cannot come from outside. If so, then this is dependent, fragile happiness, which will soon turn into sadness. Then, you will be swallowed up in a "net" of accusations and guilt, regrets and "persecution." Your happiness is interconnected with your presence, with your connection with your breath, with your body, with the "earth". Your happiness is not small, and it cannot be "removed" by fear, anger, or even the most intense shame

6.

Your happiness is not a state, not a passing experience, not an experience, and not a feeling that others can give you. Your happiness is the boundless, omnipresent, unlimited space of the heart, in which joy and sadness, bliss and melancholy, confidence and doubt, loneliness and "connectedness," even fear and strong desire, can replace each other, like rainy and sunny weather." - Jeff Foster

7.
"To get rid of anxiety about a reality that you cannot change, you need to accept it. And then it, this inconvenient reality, will leave you alone. What does it mean to accept? And why can you get rid of annoying problems in this way? Because when you accept, you stop worrying and caring. As long as it touches you, you "don't let go" and broadcast it in the mirror. The mirror always reflects the way you think. As soon as you accept it, it leaves the image and, accordingly, disappears from the reality around you." - Vadim Zeland

8.
"Abandon worry, desire and hope. Leave only calm confidence. Feel this state of intention to get what you want, without any conditions or reasoning. For example, I don't think about whether I'll be on time, whether the bus will come, how long I'll have to wait... - I just go to the stop and know that the bus will come now. Let this state accompany you everywhere." Vadim Zeland

Thank you!

I want to believe that this book was useful and helps you in your life, like the moral support of a good friend, in some ways it encourages you, in others it will give you advice, in others it will make you think.

The material for this book took a long time to collect, and it was created out of inspiration, out of nowhere, from the desire to make a book of exactly this format in a matter of weeks

Thank you very much for your help in creating this book, Leslie Harwood.

Our Published Books

THE POCKET ORACLE

Welcome to TheHappyStoryGarden!

www.ingramcontent.com/pod-product-compliance
Lightning Source LLC
Chambersburg PA
CBHW050146130526
44591CB00033B/699